The Introvert's Advantage

The Introverts Guide To Succeeding In An Extrovert World

By Michele Gilbert

<u>Visit My Amazon Author Page</u>

Dedicated to those who choose to stretch beyond their own limits

and to seek a more abundant and fulfilling life.

Your thoughts are creative.

Michele Gilbert

Table of contents

Introduction

I want to thank you and congratulate you for downloading the book, *"The Introvert's Advantage"*.

This book contains proven steps and strategies on how to succeed in an extrovert world.

Are you an introvert? You're in good company. If all the introverts got together (a thought that would horrify us), you'd find nearly half of the population are introverts. Some introverts are famous and have lived extremely public lives. Some don't even know they are introverted.

You probably chose this book because you want to learn how to become an extrovert. There is a general belief that extroverts are happier, more sociable, better adjusted and much more popular.

The *bad* news is that you can't change your personality type.

The *good* news is that you don't need to. Introverts actually have the advantage. We are statistically brighter, better in many workplace environments, and can put on a peacock display which will knock the spots off an extrovert. The trick is learning your strengths and putting them to work.

And *that* is the best reason for buying this book.

So are you ready?

Then let the journey begin...

So What Is An Introvert Anyway

The main difference between introverts and extroverts is not in their public behaviour, but in the way they recharge their batteries. Introverts need a lot of alone time, but when they do strut their stuff they can do it as well as any extrovert.

You may have assumed the shy quiet person in the corner is an introvert, but that the one in the middle of the room making all the noise is definitely an extrovert. Actually, they may both be introverts. People genuinely don't always know themselves that they have an introvert personality type!

Check the chapter on Introverts versus Extroverts, but if you listen when you are told things, prefer small groups to large parties, and relax with a book or watching a favourite film, you are an introvert. Congratulations! Introverts dominate the gifted section of the community. It is far easier to learn social confidence than to learn how to cope without the restless need for constant stimulation.

The Common Misconceptions Of Introverts

The most common misconception is that all introverts have social anxieties. Actually, both introverts and extroverts may have social anxieties. We just cope with them differently. They certainly aren't a defining factor.

Contrary to what most people think, a shy person is certainly an introvert, but not all introverts are shy.

Neither do we find it difficult to have conversations. We just find small talk pointless. Interesting conversations about ideas and concepts? Now you're talking.

This leads to another misconception, that we are awkward and rude. An introvert trying to shake off a relentless extrovert may eventually have to be rude. That is something you can work on, because they don't like it!

Here are some other common misconceptions:

Introversion is a personality disorder. No, to be introvert (or extrovert) is a personality type, not a disorder. Extremes of both types are discussed in the next chapter.

Introverts don't like people. We do. We like our friends very much indeed. We just don't consider every stranger a friend we don't yet know.

Introverts don't go out in public. We do. Public is fine. If there's a point to it.

Introverts prefer to be alone. No, not *prefer*. But being alone is how we recharge. And we don't like being with people just for the sake of being with people.

Introverts don't know how to relax and have fun. Are you kidding? We just don't need to be making a noise or in the middle of a crowd to be having fun. We can do that, and enjoy it, but we don't need it.

Introverts can become extroverts. No, we can't. We can learn to be extroverted in public, but we can't become extroverts. On the other hand, we are thinkers, makers, doers, and we can be performers. Why would we want to change that?

Introvert versus Extrovert

There's a temptation to be rude about extroverts because they're unlikely ever to read this book. They're not big readers. However, this is not, nor should ever be, a case of Them versus Us. Apart from anything else, there are very few pure extroverts and introverts. Most of us combine traits of both. A few are so equally balanced they are called ambiverts; comfortable with groups and social interaction, but also relishing time alone, away from a crowd.

Opposites attract. Most successful relationships (personal and professional) combine the two types. Two true introverts would never meet. Two true extroverts would never stop talking long enough to notice each other.

We react differently to different situations. In a crisis, even an introvert may run in circles shouting, which is a very extroverted thing to do. There is a definite point to finding out your dominant personality type, though. It can point you in a different direction workwise, and help you find a job truly suited to your talents. It can help you recognise and work around your social attitudes. Looking for the extroverted traits in your introverted nature helps you make the most of them, in a culture that makes an approving fuss of extroverts.

Recognizing your introverted traits helps you benefit from them instead of pushing yourself to be something you are not. People don't always know they are introverted, especially if they have misconceptions about the type. If you're looking forward to the weekend as a time to recharge after a busy week, do you look forward most to the planned get-together on Saturday night, or to the lazy morning beforehand? Extroverts recharge from the company of others. Introverts recharge from time alone.

An extrovert is restless and bored without people around, and time spent alone is to be endured and kept as brief as possible. An introvert actively enjoys having a sleep-in, kicking back and relaxing between social engagements.

Pop round on a surprise visit to an extrovert at nine in the morning on a Sunday, and they will practically drag you into the house. An introvert will hesitate before answering the door, even though they end up enjoying the visit. Some introverts even screen their phone calls. They'll call back, even immediately, but they like to engage gear first.

Introverts find small talk irritating. Extroverts don't like talking seriously.

Introverts go to parties to catch up with people they already know, rather than to meet new people. Extroverts are delighted to find they hardly recognize anyone in the room.

Introverts can find themselves feeling bored or even lonely in a crowd of people, even people they know and like. Getting back home and kicking off their shoes to unwind seems more attractive by the minute. Extroverts are astonished at the idea. They can agree the talk is boring, the music is too loud, and that some of the other guests are becoming drunk and belligerent, but they would still rather be there than alone at home.

Introverts like to discuss books and thought-provoking films, and are taken aback when people (i.e. extroverts) accuse them of being intense. Extroverts can remember who they saw the film with, but rarely remember the philosophical message, unless that seems important to their peer group. Then they will be able to mention it with assurance. They still won't want to analyze it in an in-depth conversation, though.

Introverts like a productive work environment. Having a radio playing loudly, a stream of visitors, or a video screen in the office, is a constant distraction. To extroverts, it is an ideal workplace.

Introverts become tired in noisy social situations because they want to understand everything going on around them. Too much activity is draining.

However, introverts are often very good public speakers, and speaking to a large audience doesn't worry them. A surprising number of performers—actors, singers, politicians—are introverts. The meet-and-greet afterwards, though, is a trial, while to the extrovert it is the reward for gathering all those people together.

Introverts don't like to be hemmed in by people. Faced with sitting at a long table, or on the subway, they will sit at one end, not in the middle. In a cinema or theatre, they are happiest in the aisle seat.

Introverts like to be in relationships with extroverts, who not only encourage them to get out and about more, but can take up the social slack when the introvert is flagging.

Introverts would rather be good at a few things than Jack of all trades. They can focus better than extroverts, and cope better with intense study.

Introverts notice more, and draw conclusions, where extroverts can be oblivious.

Introverts feel crushed and uncomfortable in a huge crowd. Extraverts feel energized and excited.

Introvert children are told to participate more in class. Extrovert children are told to stop being disruptive.

Introverts are often writers, preferring to communicate in a way where they can arrange their words to say exactly what they mean. Extroverts are more likely to be good at marketing and selling – another partnership which can be brilliantly successful.

Introverts can be the life and soul of a party or group holiday, or a vocal and active member of a work-team, but they need to balance those bursts of energy with recovery time. They become stressed when the pressure is ongoing and recovery time, especially expected recovery time, is disrupted.

Introverts are self-aware, thoughtful, and observant. They like learning new things, and watching rather than taking center stage. Many introverts are spouses to successful extroverts, and contribute to that success with their complementary skills.

Introverts have a smaller group of friends than extroverts, admitting new friends only after due consideration, and they value them highly. Socially, they prefer dinner parties to huge social gatherings.

Introverts tend to think about things before offering an opinion, while extroverts talk first, and learn through trial and error.

The need for occasional solitude to recharge is a strength, not a weakness. We emerge from recharges stronger and more able than before, capable of anything we have resolved to do.

Introverts are reticent about sharing personal information.

Introverts understand extroverts. Extroverts do not understand introverts.

Advantages of Introverts And Why You May Want To Be One

You probably realized in the previous chapter that being introverted has definite advantages. Not only can we act as extrovert as a boisterous world could want (so long as we have enough downtime to recharge) we have some serious strengths of our own which no extrovert could adopt.

When it comes to friends, we can claim quality rather than quantity.

Statistically, we have lower blood pressure.

We have the skills to cope with isolation and solitude – situations that would drive extroverts crazy.

Because we don't rush into speech to fill every silence, what we do say is usually worth listening to.

We have the ability to look inward and evaluate ourselves. This can give us the blueprint for moving forward. Learning from mistakes, especially the mistakes of others, is an advantage many true extroverts will never have. *Use* this ability to identify your key strengths: then develop a plan which uses them and supports the things you are best at.

Introverts like thinking and learning. Turn that to advantage. Learn the things that will advance your skills.

Introverts get the job done, and they get it done properly. They often improve on the way it was being done! Make sure you are in a role that suits your talents, however. A role which calls for non-stop interaction and force of personality will become increasingly stressful. Leave sales, public relations, any role where you need to constantly meet and influence new people, to the extroverts. Supporting those roles, or a job where you can work with a degree of independence, is a far better fit. Any job that rewards your ability to learn and improve is also a good choice. Doctors, accountants, computer programmers, or those in creative fields, are nearly always introverts.

Extroverts turn the wheels and introverts supply the grease. In fact our main problem has never been what we do, and how we do it; it has been in underlining our contribution. We work quietly, and are often only truly appreciated after we leave our jobs.

The chapter on being a comfortable introvert in an extrovert world looks at improving that situation. There are a fair few famous introverts who have quietly moved to the very top of their professions. It comes down to doing what you do best, so well that it becomes impossible to ignore. And learning a few social skills. We are *very* good at learning.

Being A Comfortable Introvert In An Extroverted World

Extraverts are everywhere. It isn't so much that they outnumber us, because the split might be as near as fifty / fifty, especially with all the extroverted introverts out there. They are simply more visible! You can use them to your advantage – because extraverts always want to talk and network you can give them something to talk about: you. Find yourself an extravert who knows your talents and get them to sell you to everyone else.

Never forget that extroverts thrive on an audience and a good extrovert / introvert partnership benefits both. Extroverts can sell a concept, introverts can deliver. The extrovert will usually be the public face of the partnership. As long as the partnership is privately considered equal by both parties, that's an ideal situation.

We can be extroverted in public, but we would burn ourselves out if we tried to do it as a permanent lifestyle. The trick is to pace yourself. Always plan your recharge time, and stick to it. If your pressure levels are high, learn to meditate: twenty minutes of meditation can, at a pinch, replace two hours of private downtime; and it is far easier to find twenty minutes in a crowded schedule.

Background noise is becoming the norm. You *have* to schedule quiet times, but with those in place, you will cope.

If you want to start building your extroverted skills, you'll find it easy enough if you start sensibly. Don't decide you have to get over your shyness by booking a hectic group holiday with strangers. Small steps will give you confidence. If you're waiting in a queue at the supermarket, strike up a mini conversation with the next person in the queue. Maybe they have a type of hot drink you haven't tried, among their purchases. Ask if they are trying it, or whether they buy it regularly. It isn't small talk if it is something you would genuinely like to try. Smile a goodbye as you go through the till. If they are extroverts, they will be delighted to chat. If they are introverted, it isn't small talk—you are genuinely interested, and they will have an opinion to share.

OK, that's an extreme example and you are probably well past that stage already, but my point is that small undemanding moments of reaching out won't be difficult, and will give you confidence with strangers. Contacts don't have to be verbal. The train delayed? Someone is rolling their eyes and trying to catch your attention? Smile back. Empathy.

Extroverts *love* listeners. Nod, smile, say 'oh yes!' or 'really?' and they will consider you the most charming and delightful person they met that day.

What every introvert dreads is attracting a true relentless extrovert who, once connected, won't let go, and won't stop talking even though they aren't *saying* anything. Confidence-building experiments should always be in a situation where you have an escape route, and life is *filled* with those.

Don't, for example, strike up a conversation with the person next to you at the start of a four hour journey. If they start one with you, smile and be noncommittal and get out your book. You can exchange smiles and the lightest of social comments at intervals, once you have established you have a book to get back to!

Remember also that you don't *have* to talk. What every *extrovert* dreads is being stuck in a conversation with someone who feels much more strongly than they do, on a subject they don't find interesting, who is keeping them away from other people they could be meeting.

Don't hang around too long generally, extroverts want an ever-changing audience. Move away charmingly ('I need to get a drink', or 'I'm so sorry, I have a report to get out or I'll be hauled over the coals'.)

If you are in a group environment, introduce the extrovert to someone you know, or pull another guest into the conversation and then smilingly detach yourself. Leave them wanting more.

Part of being comfortable in an extroverted world is to realize that your role, except with your true friends, is to be a listener, not a talker. Once you have become a good listener your popularity will become, well, overwhelming.

At work, listen to your manager (I know you do anyway, but smile, look impressed as you scribble a note) and without pealing with laughter at his or her jokes, show appreciation. Socially, the ability to look fascinated is irresistible. Disagree by all means, but make it a laughing protest, not a flat stare. As your confidence grows, contribute your own comments because it is a little unnerving, except for a full-on extrovert, to talk to someone who listens politely but never responds.

Social popularity doesn't condemn you to a lifelong role as a listener; many introverts have been famous leaders, either in their field or in public life. Listening is, however, part of their strength and why they are remembered with great respect.

Some environments are more challenging than others. Increasingly popular buzzwords like 'interactive' and 'teambuilding' can strike a cold chill to introverts at school and work. There is more focus on being seen to do the job, than on doing the job properly, which is frankly bewildering to an introvert. How do you work around that?

For starters, don't accept impossible deadlines. If you are given a job which you privately estimate should take two or three hours (or days, or weeks), promise you'll do everything in your power to get it done in four. If your manager wants it in one, shake your head ruefully and say you can't do it properly in the time. Do *not* hurry away feeling stressed and turn in substandard work, which will stress you more. Far better to get a reputation as someone who delivers on the promises (slightly ahead of time) than as someone who misses deadlines, or fails to deliver at all.

If you haven't a clue how long a job will take, be confident about saying you'll look at it and come back with a time estimate. Don't feel pressured to come up with an answer, and try to avoid saying 'I don't know'. Saying 'I'll get back to you about that' is more positive. It also emphasizes the point that you are a thinker and a doer. If the person asking is impatient and presses, *smile,* rather than looking harassed, and set a time. Ten minutes. An hour. By the end of the day, whichever. Get back to them within the promised time.

When you know a brainstorm meeting is coming up, ask your manager for a heads up and make the point that you like to put in a bit of thought ahead of time. This is a virtue. Present it as such. This is one time you can't get away with being purely a listener. Have two or three ideas on hand, look enthusiastic when extrovert colleagues jump in, and if they've completely missed the point say something on the lines of, 'that wasn't quite where I was heading, but that's an interesting take'. Even if it isn't. This comes back to letting extroverts talk for you, and once they *have* got the point you can leave it to them to push it through. They may not even remember where the idea came from, but your manager should. Even so, keep track of the ideas that work out well, and mention them in your next assessment. Even if they have evolved almost beyond recognition, your idea was the original spark.

Group projects are a bit of a minefield. The extroverts talk a great deal and disagree boisterously, and the introverts have to deliver, knowing exactly who will get the credit. Try to isolate something you know you can do well and offer to take it on and bring it back for input.

Expect your ideas to be run off with. That's your value to a team. Rescue them if you can. If you can't, accept that getting annoyed when they are twisted out of shape will bewilder the extroverts. If management like the ideas, that's what counts. Quietly keep ownership of them, and openly credit those who changed them to their present status. They will be more likely to become your vocal supporters and interested in your future ideas.

A good manager is someone who can spark both ideas and development, and many introverts who become recognized as a good source of ideas or support become excellent managers, who can keep a good overall grasp of the big picture and use team strengths to maximum effect.

Introvert managers will tend to work to an agenda, with specifics that must be raised. Within that framework, they will often draw a far better performance from the team than someone with fixed end result they can't or won't relinquish. Sometimes it helps introverts in a team to take step back and analyze (another introvert skill) what the end result should be, then mentally assign tasks. It can make the overall project, and even the way it has been allocated, much easier to understand.

An important part of working successfully in an extroverted environment is to care about what you're doing, and let your enthusiasm show. Whether you get your way or not, the extroverts will identify with your passion, if it doesn't turn into stubborn intensity. Learning when to let go, and when to insist, is the *successful* introvert's greatest skill.

Use your past record, don't let it be overlooked. Have a website, a body of work, some way of keeping your successes visible even if it is only regular work reviews. Keep track of every success, and make your record work for you.

Performing in an extrovert world requires acting skills and it is no coincidence that many famous performers are introverts. Standing up in front of others, whether to present an idea or a show, is easier when you divorce yourself from your shyness and concentrate on turning in an intelligent, insightful acting job.

Know your comfort levels and work around them. If you need regular breaks to be alone, take them. Stressing and exhausting yourself isn't good for you and isn't good for your employer. If your job requires seeing people one after the other, build in ten minutes between meetings. Get away from your desk regularly. Your lunch break is sacred. Head to a park, for instance, or read a book. Head to the local shops, at worst, for a change in environment and away from the need to be sociable. This is recharge time, to get you back to peak performance for the afternoon.

Don't feel obliged to attend work-related social events if you dread them. A vague 'oh, I can't do this Friday, what a pity' will get you out of most. If they happen every Friday, accept occasionally as if you simply can't resist, 'even though I can't stay late'.

Most of the comments in this chapter were about working environments, and relate also to schools and academic environments. For social and dating tips, see that chapter.

You Are Not Alone...Famous Introverts

It is encouraging to know how many household names are as much introverts as you and I. These are all people who have juggled being in the limelight with needing quiet time, in a world that watches extroverts.

The list is far from definitive, because I only included names where they are either on record describing themselves as introverted, or appeared on at least five lists. I checked exhaustively because some of the names definitely surprised me.

Entertainers like Julia Roberts, Lady Gaga, Christina Aguilera, David Letterman, Gwyneth Paltrow, Harrison Ford, Audrey Hepburn, Candice Bergen, Tom Hanks, and Johnny Carson.

Public figures like Abraham Lincoln, Eleanor Roosevelt (who was also an American spokesperson in the United Nations after being a very public wife), Laura Bush, and Clint Eastwood (who of course also qualifies on the above list).

Successful super-rich businesspeople like Bill Gates and Warren Buffet.

Household names like Charles Darwin, JK Rowling, Albert Einstein, Mahatma Gandhi, Rosa Parks, Stephen Spielberg and Alfred Hitchcock.

Pretty good company we're keeping.

Dating Tips And Introverts In Love

Single introverts don't *have* to date, and we are certainly perfectly happy on our own. However, *homo sapiens* is a sociable and gregarious species and we are all happiest when we have family, friends, and are loved by someone we love in return.

Introverts *can* become reclusive and that in time can lead to depression. Push yourself to socialize a bit more if you realize you are spending more time alone with every year that passes. It can be hard to reverse but we can otherwise reach a point where there is too much recharge, and not enough discharge. That's not good for anyone, whatever their personality type.

Whether you are looking to date for the first time, or starting over, the most daunting challenge for an introvert is: where are the best places to meet people? When you find large social groups exhausting, small talk annoying, and are a little shy with strangers, it can be a problem. So where do you start looking?

The ideal is to be introduced to eligible types by **friends** at an enjoyable sociable occasion, and explore mutual interest without any direct pressure. The trouble is that once your friends realize you're looking, they eagerly produce people of every type and watch with avid interest. Rather tell your friends you want to meet new people and get out more, and they are likely to include you in invitations they may otherwise have thought wouldn't interest you.

Looking online has advantages and disadvantages. The advantages are pretty good: you can look for people in your area who share at least some of your interests, and learn some basics about them before setting up that first meeting. You also know they are equally keen to meet someone. The disadvantages are the alarming number of scammers and chancers. It can feel you're the only genuine person on there. You aren't. Don't fall for any hard-luck stories, accept that anyone who sounds too good to be true is probably lying, and generally be cautious. Chat through the website, don't hurry to offer or give out your contact details and don't trust anyone who is too quick with theirs.

Take a class in something that interests you; a new language, a hobby like photography or car maintenance, or a keep-fit option like yoga or martial arts. At the very least you will make new friends with shared interests. A cooking or wine appreciation class leads to social get-togethers. Drawing classes are particularly satisfying; few introverts realize how creative they are.

Join a group for dog-walking, or writing, or perhaps a book club, to have built-in conversational topics with the people you meet.

Volunteering is also a good way to meet people who share your passions: politics, animal shelters, local history, tend to attract volunteers who feel deeply about the same things as you do. That makes starting and sharing conversations remarkably easy.

Bite the bullet and socialize. There are ways of being approachable, rather than having to make the first move, and they range from the obvious to the subtle.

- Dress to impress the types you want to meet. Go for a look that feels right to you – no point in looking entirely unlike yourself, unless you intend to change your look permanently. For example, if you usually wear your hair scraped back, is going with elaborate ringlets the ideal way to set up your first impression with someone you hope to meet again?

- Look good, though. Your party look can by all means hint at the fact you are an outdoors type; wear jeans and a shirt if that's your style, rather than a frilly dress. Just make sure the jeans fit well and the top flatters you.

- Washed hair, brushed teeth, no BO or bad breath, is as attractive to anyone else as it would be to you. We are genetically attracted to people who look healthy and well-maintained.

- Don't plaster on makeup, or use too heavy a scent—whisper, don't shout.

- Once you're there, relax. Be interested in your surroundings. *Don't* be engrossed in your phone or book; you'll look as though you don't want to be interrupted.

- If you're with friends, don't turn your back on the room or focus only on the people you are with already. Smile, listen, chat, but also look around with interest.

- Don't go on the hunt with your guy friends. *No* man is going to try an approach in front of other men.

- If you make eye contact with someone who looks interesting, glance back occasionally. Carry on looking round at others. There are two ways of eye flirting—opening your eyes slightly wider, holding it for a couple of seconds, then smiling and looking away; or quick glances, looking away as soon as you see he's watching. Smiling to yourself will tell him you're interested. He may not be available, just enjoying a mild eye flirt. Enjoy it yourself, without being downcast if he doesn't follow up.

- Don't focus all your attention on the promising guy over in the corner who is enjoying the attention but not coming over. There may be someone else watching you.

- Make it easier for him to talk to you, especially if you're with friends. Walk away from your group for a few minutes to look around, or get a breath of fresh air, or go order a drink at the bar.

- Don't look bored. Interested people look more interesting.

- Don't be rude, mocking, or use foul language, unless that is the type you want to attract. Be the sort of person you'd like to meet.

- Body language says a lot about you. Smiling, straightening your back, looking interested in what is going on, sends a far stronger message to a stranger than we realize.

- Look around at others, and see how you react to the way they are sitting, talking, reacting to others, to see exactly what I mean.

Where to go on a date

So you met someone, and they're suggesting meeting up again, but asking you what you'd like. If you're shy, try to avoid dinner for two on the first date. Instead, go for something which will fill any conversational gaps nicely.

- A **music café**, if you both like music, gets conversation going.

- An **art exhibition**, ditto.

- A **movie**. A sexy movie on a first date can be embarrassing—suggest a comedy or thriller you were planning to see anyway.

If, on the other hand, he suggests the sort of date that would horrify you, maybe taking a crowded train to watch a sold-out football game, when you don't even like football, don't be afraid to say that isn't your thing. If you can't decide on something you both like, there's no point in dating anyway. The relationship will never float.

What to talk about

Once the ice-breaking effects of the venue are exhausted, what next?

If you're feeling shy, admit it. Keep your body language open, smile, look towards your date; no hunted glances at the door or getting too engrossed in others at the next table.

Introverts are great listeners, so get him talking. If he's an introvert, he'll be grateful for your conversational leads: if he's an extrovert, he'll be delighted to talk on any subject. Listen and react to the answers and there you are – conversation.

Questions like 'where did you go on your last holiday' or 'is there anywhere you've ever wanted to visit' are usually good starters. If you're at an Italian café, for example, that's an absolute gift 'Have you been to Italy?' And off you go.

Other questions could include 'are you a dog or cat person' or 'do you have a big family' as long as holding up your end would be positive. Asking about favourite books or films can lead to good interaction, but change direction if his answer is something that leaves you cold. It isn't a job interview – don't fire questions. Let him come up with a few. A silence, with a shared smile, can be peaceful, not awkward. Breathe. Glance around.

Stick to a couple of drinks. One or two should relax you, too many could put you under the table or morose, or hectoring. Don't be tempted to keep drinking, even if it does give you initial confidence. Getting drunk is never a good start.

Introverts find the early stages of friendships, let alone relationships, trying. It takes time to build rapport, but if the common ground is there, it will come. The thing to remember is that an extrovert is quite happy to talk about himself to an interested listener, and an introvert understands exactly how you feel.

Relax. Enjoy. And well done for getting out there. Every time you do this, it gets easier. You won't meet the perfect match on the first try, and you will meet some extremely imperfect ones. That's life, and this is a learning curve.

Having said all that, there are some dating traps introverts can find themselves getting into. Introverts are givers, not takers. Do that self-analysis thing you do so well. Are you doing all the giving? Are you happy with the balance of the relationship, or is it all his way?

Don't be so good a listener that you never get a chance to speak. *Especially* speak up if you feel you're not getting enough recharge time, or being constantly teased about not being a party animal.

Be who you are, not who you think he wants you to be, or you will find the relationship draining and your confidence severely knocked when (not if) it ends. There's an element of adjustment in every relationship, that's to be expected, but if you have to live permanently outside your comfort levels, you won't be happy.

Don't suffer in silence and hope things will right themselves in time. Talk things through and if you can't reach agreement, you have two choices; be generally miserable for the rest of the relationship, or be briefly very miserable on your own before you start looking again, sadder but wiser.

Extroverts Defined

An extrovert is defined as a person who is energized by being around other people. Extrovert's flag and fade when alone and can easily become bored without other people around. An extrovert would rather talk with someone uncongenial than sit alone and think. In fact, extroverts often think best when they are talking.

Carl Jung defined extroversion (or extraversion) as the ability to turn the interests and energies of one's mind toward events, people, and things in the surroundings.

However, being an extrovert is not just about socializing. It is also about interacting with people around, i.e., sharing your ideas with them and being open to their ideas. Extroverts are usually enthusiasts who believe yesterday is gone, tomorrow has yet to dawn, so live for today. This can have a devastating effect on life decisions or lead to disastrous errors with long-term repercussions.

Extroverts constantly need people around, and are happy to have an ever-changing group of companions. They make the most of the opportunities coming their way without worrying about the consequences. Their tendency to say whatever they think can offend people at times.

Being gregarious and expressive, extroverts are adept in romantic relationships, especially at the start. On the flip side, however, they also find it very easy to end relationships and move on without a backward glance.

They can be a little moody and erratic, starting a task with enthusiasm and discarding it the next day. Their bad moods, because they are so expressive, are very obvious.

It would be wrong to say extroverts are poor listeners, or that they are always happy. However, it is generally true they generally enjoy fast-paced careers and are generally optimistic and persuasive, with a wide social circle.

Conclusion

Basically, everybody has both introvert and extrovert personality traits in them, and success lies i
developing the traits that will bring success, and working around the ones that will bring failure
Forming relationships in work, play and family with others with complementary traits is the secre
of truly succeeding.

I hope this book was able to help you to plan your future.

The next step is to succeed brilliantly!

Before you go, I'd like to say thank you for purchasing my book.

I know you could have picked so many other books to read on understanding introverts. But you
took a chance on me.

So A Big thanks for downloading this book and reading it all the way to completion.

Now I would like to ask a _small_ favor.

Could you please take a minute or two to leave a review for this book on Amazon?

Click here

The feedback will help me continue to publish more kindle books that will help people to ge
better results in their lives.

And if you found it helpful in anyway then please let me know :-)

Thank you and good luck!

To your success,

Michele

Preview of My New Book

The Verbal And Emotional Abuser: Recognizing The Verbal Abusive Relationship And How To Defend Yourself

CHAPTER 1
Understanding an Abuser

Humans are complicated and complex beings. From the very moment of our birth, we interact with countless other people. How we turn out as unique individuals is a result of numerous unseen factors like genetics and subtle environmental cues. We also are shaped by the social environments in which we grow and mature. Which one of these factors affects our development more is a matter of contention among psychologists and scientists alike. The nature v. nurture argument shows no sign of letting up anytime soon. These essential realities of our identity and how we become who we are cannot be denied.

However, sometimes an individual, for a myriad of reasons, can evolve into an abusive person. It is a well-established fact that many abusive individuals are products of abuse themselves. David M. Allen, M.D. says "While it is important to realize that not all abusers were abused as children, and that many if not most people who are abused do not go on to become abusers themselves, child abuse is most likely the single largest factor - biological, psychological, or sociological - for later adult abusive behavior." In this respect, many abusers are victims of abuse and cannot be judged without keeping that simple fact in mind.

If someone close to you is verbally abusive, then there is a strong likelihood that at some point during their life they experienced physical, verbal, emotional, or sexual abuse. If you are in a position to do so, it might be beneficial to discover more about why the abuser close to you behaves in the manner in which they do. They may be reluctant to open up to you about these experiences, as the experiences have caused them a lot of trauma and pain. If they are open to the possibility, then suggest seeing a therapist. If they are willing to seek professional help, then be supportive in their pursuit to find healing. But if your attempts to understand the abuser close to you are fruitless, and they are unwilling to seek professional help, then the only thing left to understand is how abusers become the abusive individuals they are.

Although abuse during childhood is a common trait of abusive individuals, as mentioned before, it is not present on every case of an abusive individual. However, just because an abuser wasn't abused physically doesn't mean there wasn't any dysfunction in their upbringing. Familial dysfunction can manifest in many various forms. For example, emotional abuse can be very subtle and hard to spot. Furthermore, subtle emotional abuse can sometimes be repressed or difficult to remember. Emotional abuse is not always as obvious as yelling, insulting, or threatening speech. Emotional abuse can take the form of passive-aggressive speech, unhealthy comparisons ("You're not as pretty as your sister" or "If only you were as smart as your brother"), or even emotional neglect.

Abusive manifestations like these, especially passive aggressive speech and emotional neglect can take their toll on a young child. But they may not have a conscious bearing on their mind. Or in other words, these abusive behaviors may have been interpreted by the abused as normal behavior. In fact, they may blame themselves for this behavior. This self-blame is true for the physically abused, as well. It is important to understand abuse as a cycle. Abuse is a cycle that often repeats itself. It may change forms or focus, however. For example, an abused child may continue the cycle of abuse during adulthood, but not by abusing another, but by abusing themselves in the form of alcohol or drug abuse and self-harm. Knowing all this, it is possible that even the abuser in your life is willing to talk to you about the abusive experiences in their past, they may not know the full extent of the abuse.

If this is the case, then the best strategy is to try to understand as much as possible about the nature of their upbringing. How was their relationship with their parents? Often, abusive individuals were influenced negatively by the presence of a narcissistic individual. Due to the controlling and emotionally manipulative qualities of a narcissist, children raised by narcissists are sometimes subjected to emotional or physical abuse. However, it is important to note that not every narcissist is physically, or even emotionally, abusive. There are a multitude of personality disorders that a parent or close loved-one might have that could contribute to a child's abusive behavior later in life.

Unfortunately, you don't have to be a narcissist or have a personality disorder to cause damage in a child's life- the kind of damage that goes on to influence their actions as abusers. Neglecting a child emotionally, while not necessarily abusive, can be very detrimental to a child and can contribute to later abusive behavior. So, what is neglect? Well, neglect can be as simple as not acknowledging the child's importance. For the neglectful parent, they can simply not put a priority on the time they spend, if it exists at all, with their children. People who spend more time in the office than with their children can put their children at risk for emotional immaturity. This immaturity can preclude them towards being abuse. However, don't forget that some parents are intentionally neglectful and make it a point to disregard their children's emotional needs. In these cases especially, a child's emotional development can shed light on why they have become abusers themselves.

Without a doubt, an abusers childhood and upbringing have a lot to do with why they behave in an abusive manner. However, childhood abuse is not the only source for an abusive individual's behavior. Drug and alcohol abuse are significant factors, as well. There are also many factors like genetics, hormonal imbalances, or even nutritional deficiencies that can increase aggressive behavior. However, every individual is different. As mentioned elsewhere, each of these common traits of an abusive individual could be present in someone who has never engaged in abusive behavior. All in all, what distinguishes an abuser is their abusive behavior that is directed towards themselves or others.

CHAPTER 2

The Consequences of Abuse

Understanding why someone might behave in an abusive manner is the first step toward liberating yourself from these individuals. If your partner is the abusive individual, then there is an added level of urgency to the matter. However, in situations such as these, it is not merely enough to understand why or how they became abusers. It is equally, if not more important, to understand what happens to ourselves as a recipient of abuse at the hands of our partner or someone close to you.

Click Here To Check Out The Rest Of

The Verbal And Emotional Abuser: Recognizing The Verbal Abusive Relationship And How To Defend Yourself

P.S. You'll find many more books like this and others under my name Michele Gilbert.

Don't miss them… here is a short list.

Stop Playing Mind Games: How To Free Yourself Of Controlling And Manipulating Relationships

Instant Charisma: A Quick And Easy Guide To Talk, Impress, And Make Anyone Like You

Chakras: Understanding The 7 Main Chakras For Beginners: The Ultimate Guide To Chakra Mindfulness, Balance and Healing

Practicing Mindfulness: Living in the moment through Meditation: Everyday Habits and Rituals to help you achieve inner peace

Sleep Tight: Overcome Insomnia and Sleep Disorders for a better more restful sleep!

Stop Back Pain Now!: Back Pain Remedies and Treatments so you can live a pain free life!

The Arthritis Pain Cure: How to find Arthritis Pain Relief and live a happy pain free life!

The Headache Pain Cure: How to find Headache Pain Relief and live a happy Pain Free Life!

Stop Panic Attacks and Anxiety Disorders without Drugs Now!: Overcome Panic, Stress and Anxiety and live a happy pain free life!

The Breakup Recovery Guide: Advice for Surviving Heartbreak, Letting Go and Thriving in an exciting new life!

The Friendship Guide to Finding Friends Forever: How to Find, Make and Keep Quality Friendships After your Breakup

The Credit Fix: Leave behind credit card debt and poor credit scores and get your life back!

How To Stop Being Jealous And Insecure: Overcome Insecurity And Relationship Jealousy

Michele Gilbert was born and raised in Brooklyn, New York. Drawn to literature and writing at a young age she enrolled at Brooklyn College and majored in English. After graduation Michele did not begin writing immediately, instead she embarked on a career in the finance industry and spent the next thirty years on Wall Street.

Serendipity struck when she least expected it. After ending a long-term relationship, Michele found herself lost and unsure what the future held. She began to read books on grief and loss, looking for answers. Those led her to delve deeper into the Law of Attraction and its power. What resulted was remarkable. Not only had she begun to heal, she had also rekindled her former love of writing and discovered her life's purpose.

The years have taken her through many twists and turns, but she learned valuable lessons along the way. Today she publishes books-mostly self-help and metaphysical in nature-and feels compelled to share her knowledge with those facing similar experiences. Her greatest hope is to inspire others and show them ways to overcome adversity and gracefully accept life's inevitable low points.

Going forward, she plans to incorporate more teachings of self-help, finance and meditation. Regular meditation is very beneficial to her progress as she forges a new life. Morning rituals and positive incantations are other practices Michele embraces; they are very restorative in daily life.

As an avid hiker, Michele and fellow club members often hike the picturesque Jersey Pine Barrens. She is a history buff, voracious reader, baseball fanatic and a foodie. She also proudly supports Trout Unlimited-a national non-profit organization dedicated to conserving, protecting and restoring North America's Coldwater fisheries and their watersheds.

Michele currently resides forty minutes from Atlantic City and the Jersey Shore. She makes her home with a Blue Russian rescue cat named Jersey, though she isn't exactly sure who rescued who.

Michele really enjoys publishing books that can make a difference in people's lives. If you have any suggestions or would like to have a specific topic covered in a future book, please send an email to michelegilbertbooks@gmail.com and we will get back to you.

Thanks for reading!

www.ingramcontent.com/pod-product-compliance
Lightning Source LLC
Chambersburg PA
CBHW050925290526
45792CB00002B/888